Songs for God

Aloysius Sieracki,
Order of Carmelites

With drawings by Mary Ann Entrup

magnificat press
Avon-by-the-Sea, N.J.

Listing of Poems

Songs for God
The Praise of Glory
A Cancer of Pain
Places in the Heart
Earthbound
My Twin
Little Flowers
Power and Glory
Visions
A Time for Building
Daniel
Sonnet to Stillness
The Brown Clown
Shower of Roses
Psalm 40
A Woodland Lament
To a Wounded Dove
Night
Soliloquy
My Christmas Prayer
Covenant Love
Going to the Father
The Hidden Face of God
Nonetheless a Rose
Carmel's Call

Preface

I offer this small book to you as a meditation upon God, that beautiful mystery, that unique trinity of Persons who created us, forms us and loves us so completely. The poems and the accompanying drawings and Scripture phrases furnish opportunities for us to focus our search for God and His presence in our lives. The sketches by Mary Ann Entrup were drawn upon reflection on the poems in the book, and the phrases from Scripture are in some cases intimately connected with the poems. I believe that this gives the book a unity that otherwise might not be so apparent. An underlying basis for every part of this work is God's reality in our daily lives.

St. Therese of the Child Jesus and of the Holy Face is a subject, directly or indirectly, of many of the poems. Her presence here at Aylesford, the Carmelite Center in Darien, Illinois, where I reside and work, is undeniable. The National Shrine of the Society of the Little Flower is here on the grounds, and the spirit of St. Therese, a spirit of trust, self-abandonment and spiritual childhood, seems to be always ready to envelop any person who is ready for it. The spirituality of Carmel is also felt here. It has influenced my work. Carmel issues a challenge to us to live contemplatively in today's busy world and to seek the face of God in prayer. For this reason, I have included at the end of the book an essay, "The Call to Carmel," which is in one sense a commentary on the poem "Carmel's Call." It is a call to risk everything in following Jesus Christ.

There are some empty pages in this book and I offer them as an opportunity for you, the reader, to write, compose or draw your own songs for God. We need only search within the depths of our own being to find those melodies that create a paean of praise to the God whom we love. We need only allow the time and make the effort to do so.

I give my special thanks to Mary Ann Entrup, without whose drawings this small book would not have been possible; to Patricia Gangas, who has been such an encouragement and teacher to me in my efforts to write poetry; and to the Carmelites, religious and lay, and our Monday night prayer group, who furnish inspiration and models to me in my life of prayer.

Aloysius Sieracki, O. Carm.

Songs for God

"I'll write a song"; porous lies the sand.
"and pen some scenes"; "Oompah!" mocks the drum.
"Just wait, you'll see"; "Fool!" whispers the wind.
"'Oh, my,' says I"; "Continue, my son."

"A hymn to my love"; "Shhh!" moans the snore.
"a sonata so sweet"; "Tch, tch, tch!" sound the drops.
"Beautiful curls and sweeps"; hazy paints the fog.
"'I'll stop,' says I"; "Your songs are not done."

And so I write, and so she draws,
unvarnished though the hymns may be,
a symphony amid the cacophony
of human pain and age's drain,
love arrows to the Lord.

The Praise of Glory

Surging up,
    geyser-like,
    from depths unknown,
    currents gushing forth,
    melodic in their tempo,
    reaching for the heights,
        like a gymnast,
        catapulting up,
        hands free,
while the lightning charges,
        racing through the heavens
            like a falcon in flight
            on a night of flame,
            the thunder in step,
            its tremors pealing
            a cosmic chorus.
God's creation,
        welling up
            like a flash flood
            in a precipitous canyon,
            bursting its bonds,
            overwhelming the human in its wake.
Holy,
        holy,
            holy . . .

"The One who sat on the throne said to me,

'See, I make all things new!'"

Rev. 21:5

A Cancer of Pain

Mother earth has cancer.
It contorts her face in pain,
a life drama unfolding, tragic and murky,
malignant cells spreading melancholy and despair,
giving rise to diatribes and diasporas,
multiplying, crucifying, growing everywhere,
a carcinoma of suffering.

Needed are the surgeon's scalpels
to carve away the swollen tissues
dealing death and misery.
Wanted are the penetrating rays
to burn away the dreaded tumors
causing sin to swell and goals to wane.
Longing for the potent chemistry
to keep at bay the lessening
of family, faith and fellowship.

Come, O Spirit of God,
and with love's embrace,
breathe a healing warmth
on her holy face.

"Remember,

where your treasure is,
there your heart is also."

Matt. 6:21

———————————————————————

Places in the Heart

The heart is a womb
in which is conceived
the lion who plays with the lamb,
safeguarding a path for the wounded stag.
Creating the mood
that governs the days,
it welcomes its God
with loving embrace,
restoring anew the Eden of old.

The heart is a tomb
in which are interred
the Furies who prowled in the nights,
the shackles they carried broken and spent.
By laying to rest
the cries for revenge,
it celebrates its freedom
in jubilant song,
inviting the child within to glory.

Earthbound

With wings extended wide,
and fluttering all their worth,
a little bird's in flight
and still constrained to earth.

Impeded, worse than caged,
aloft, and yet not free;
imprisoned by a web
on silken, cumbrous feet.

A dogged bird, determined bird,
desiring so to fly,
a thrust to make, a web to break,
a sunny realm the prize.

To struggle free, so good to see,
a move to disenthrall,
persistent flight from prison's night,
a lantern guiding all.

In bondage still, to soar a dream,
the prison holding fast,
and yet the hope that time will bring
a skyward course at last.

My Twin

My twin in the Lord, my friend,
spirit of like spirit,
here we are as one,
conceived by a breath of God,
born of a heart of flame,
a womb suffused with love,
its consuming fire outreaching
to each of us and to all.

Here we stand, together,
a presentation of doves,
the meager gift of the poor,
a fragrance of aloes and myrrh,
the precious ointments for burial,
a Eucharistic offering
given as bread for life.

My friend in Christ,
the Master comes
and leaves but one way to receive Him:
united as one
to troth our lives
and give them to Him for the taking,
since when we were born
the covenant was signed
with the blood of the Lamb.

Little Flowers

Lovely small flowers appearing on scene,
ignoring the fanfare of garden display;
a sensate delight if only we might
recapture the days of youth evergreen.

Bright little flowers in humble repose,
adorning asphalt, the woodlands and grass
with thistles, bells and Lazy Susan shells;
so often they're found where clear water flows.

Are these little flowers fit for a king;
for transplant to garden, a small bouquet?
Unlike lily, rose or flowers with bows,
a plain, simple charm is their special thing.

Fit for a king? Surely! It's clear to see
the care they're given by God's loving hand;
so many we're blest that He saw it best
to lavishly spread them for you and for me.

"That is my joy,
   and it is complete.
He must increase,
   while I must decrease."
                    John 3:29-30

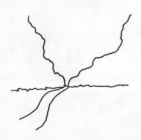

Power and Glory

Reflections on a cityscape:
a dead skunk lying on a woodland road
scenting the cars which pass its way;
idle locomotives rusting in a rail yard,
paunchy men nearby playing a game of touch;
Canada geese munching on suburban lawns,
the clouds and smoke above spawning an acid rain;
a crippled ironworker making his way,
a terrier barking at him from fear;
urban homeless huddling around a fire for warmth,
a cold open-hearth awaiting its demise;
a little child laughing heartily
in bold attempts to catch a butterfly;
Christ must increase, I must decrease;
let it be!

Visions

O Mother Mary, loudly I proclaim
exciting news of seeing you each day
in faith-enlightened visions calling me
to magnify and glorify your name.

No visions seen by me as Bernadette
at Lourdes did see and yet, I see
your beauty sketched in those with child who walk
the aisles selecting food for family needs.

Your many shrines all point to times you came;
so fitting then to dedicate the grounds
where holy Sisters pray and weary travellers stay,
for sure, in truth, they tell of thee.

The sight of you with Christ, your Son, was never
meant for me to see. Still when I view
a modern Eve beneath her cross today
in slight disguise I recognize your face.

And now no angel come to me from high;
instead, you're here and listening I reply,
"Behold a votive offering given free;
may all that you have said be done to me."

A Time for Building

No time to waste, I'm in a hurry
to see the mansion built as planned
so that its noble lord may enter
and there receive a permanent guest.

Yet it must be done with due deliberation
for works that last take time and skill.
Patiently, the schedule must be honored,
meticulously, the particulars scanned.

I don't wait as one who's foolish.
Nothing will finally be too late.
Late has been my care and late has been my planning.
More delays I will not know.

Don't speak to me of races, ventures
or family ties that do embrace.
Only cite what aids in building
for urgency now sets the pace.

Still the time will take its taking;
it isn't with my skills I build.
Nothing human lasts on making.
Needed, Lord, your timeless skill.

Then dwell within and bid me enter;
we will live together anew,
feasting, enjoying, relishing and tasting
all the delights which come from you.

Daniel

Tender is the game you play,
delicate the patterns you weave
as you screen an embraceable you
in travelling the lanes of the city.

Showing a weak side to opponents,
you turn over the myths
of saner, stronger men
by blowing the trumpet as at Jericho.

Like a high priest, you perform
the liturgies of the court,
delivering us from the lions,
laying up treasures for the king.

In tribute to eternal play,
I revel in the trumpet's song,
a simple rhythm holding sway,
a prelude to a gentler way.

"Desist!
and confess
    that I am God,...
exalted upon the earth."
                    Psalm 46:11

Sonnet to Stillness

The shaded woodland nourishes my soul.
I pause a bit to drink it in, athirst
for living waters which I sought at first
in every game I played to gain control.
A sadness breaks the spell, unleashing whole
remembrances of dreams and schemes that burst
and left a void within, myself well-versed
in enervating ways that took a toll.

With humble heart admit your poverty
and rest awhile to contemplate the view.
A likelihood you well may find it odd
enjoying gopher, lark and willow tree,
but be refreshed in seeing them anew.
Be still, my child, and know that I am God.

Clown scuplture by Jerzy Kenar

The Brown Clown

O clown, your outfit does delight,
a garb in brown of earthen hue
in shades that help compare it to
a field displayed in autumn light.

Its pieces blend to give a clue
how remnants which are commonplace
can aggregate with style and grace
and bring to birth someone like you.

In reverence paid to life's embrace,
you sore implore the face you see
to gain a smile and help set free
a laughter filling time and space.

Each day you show to all like me
a warm concern and life that's spiced
with joie de vivre and lovers' tryst,
a joyous feasting thanks to thee.

O gentle clown, by love enticed,
be faithful to your inner sight,
and realize that it's meet and right
to be a fool for sake of Christ.

Shower of Roses

Promise of Therese:
open skies release
manna hued in colors red.

Raining from on high,
petals now draw nigh
from the Lord's own flower bed.

Answering the call,
roses perfume all
thorny moments of each day.

Faith and trust here grow;
buddings clearly show
birthings of the Little Way.

Thanks for nature's bloom,
blossoms now entomb
anxious cares of darkened night.

Praise to Yahweh, praise,
days on endless days;
flowered life scenes filled with light.

"
...whom they could hear
speaking in tongues
and

glorifying God."

Acts 10:46

Psalm 40

Su bis shi rhee, a treacherous sea.
Su bis shi rhi, a plaintive cry.
Su bis shi rho, on waves I go.
Su bis shi rhum, viaticum.

Alamadi a, alamadi i,
the gifts of the day in endless supply!

Alamada tee, in heaven's decree
alamada to compels me to go
alamada tu as angels would do.
Alamada tie gives spoken reply
alamada tum of favors to come.

Su bis shi ray, su bis shi rhue,
in light of day a path pursue.

Alamada rhee, a way that can free
su bis shi rho the hold of the foe
alamada rhue and render as due
su bis shi rhi 'neath glorious sky
alamada rhum whatever may come.

Su bis shi rhee alamada rhee
su bis shi rhi alamada rhi
su bis shi rho alamada rho
su bis shi rhum alamada rhum.

A Woodland Lament

I tread through verdant woods in evening's light.
My walk and talk belie a heart aflame.
What words of longing can my love proclaim?
A timorous pas de deux invites the night.
Perhaps green lovebird's song and dance can right
the stumbling, barren efforts which I claim.
Oh, who will orchestrate my steps and tame
the glowing passions, burning, blazing bright?

Accept yourself as weakness you declare,
and let the fire's heat be your reply.
Just tend the roses blossoming through care;
an oft-repeated process passes by.
Be privy to a secret that I share:
the cry you hear is but my silent sigh.

To a Wounded Dove

O wounded dove, you ply the currents high.
Is it the scars that help you sky afar,
or svelte, lithe wings which yet no pellets mar?
Divulge your lovely secret when you're by.
Perhaps the hurts have spawned a flight awry,
which inner spirit steers where zephyrs are.
Accept our quest and fly towards nearest star
and bear us news which mysteries satisfy.

Remembering wounds which framed a fresh
    new course,
I dream of kingdoms, clowning lambs and rain
and imitate the youthful doves at play,
accepting lessons, trusting of their source,
a dove who's old, who's good at easing pain.
Come fly with me; we'll strike a brand-new day.

"The Lord
be with your spirit.
Grace be with you."
2 Tim. 4:22

Night

Alone and alert you feel the wind subside
in the darkening watch of the night.
The moon is obscured by earth
and provides no face to reflect.
All is in place.

The course of the earth is stilled
and you sense magnetic attractions
pulling you east,
as voiceless choirs sing
the forgotten songs of the past.
Desires now cease.

You float in a weightless body
and the ether's primordial airs
seem to envelop you.
The beat of your heart is constant alone,
inching you on
to the fullness of grace.

Soliloquy
(before a statue of the Sacred Heart)

Silent you stand. Are you fire? Or a lyre touched by
      heavenly winds?
Speak if you will, this much I know,
a thirst waiting to be quenched, a cup ready to be drunk,
      leaving more, still more.
And you wait to be taken up by me.

Ardent your gaze, while displaying a core of steel
softened by fire.
Clearly I see in evening's light
a flower cultured in its bloom, a soldier looking
        to the dawn, expecting more, still more.
So I stand to be forged and fired by you.

"and they shall call him
Emmanuel,'
a name which means,"
'God is with us.'
Matt. 1:23

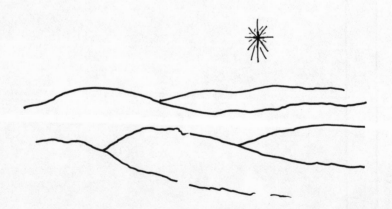

My Christmas Prayer

Mankind's love-filled vessel,
most holy Saint Therese,
pour out the good tidings
of Christmas joy and peace, ·
that born through grace is He
with whom you shared love's feast.

Merciful love victim,
O Virgin bound, yet free,
angels carol "Glory . . . "
and shepherds hastening see
in my embodied manger
love's gift betrothed to thee.

Mystic rose of Carmel,
for little souls a "way,"
like your mother Mary,
I ponder as I pray,
ready for love's promise
this coming Christmas day.

Covenant Love

Celibate passion,
receptive posture,
learning of love
in quiet of night.
Glorious mercy,
glorifying justice,
trusting all of the
Lord's design's as right.
Why is it that in the game of life I feel that I'm ahead, so far ahead?
What is it that the Lord sees in me as beautiful, worthy of love?
How can I leap into the breach to keep evil from destroying the land?
How can it happen that my body in consecration can be given up for you?
Why in Communion does the Christ in me so clearly see the Christ in you?
Lateness of hour,
life seeking light,
dark contemplation,
nascent delight.
Inspiration bright-
ening the night,
waiting for daybreak
to be proclaimed
as Good News.
Vistas opening
to be realized
in loving action.
Pleasure and pain,
each of the other,
whenever they come,
intensely, surely,
measuring life.
Treat me gently, Lord;
I know so little of love.
Tired-out body, out-
stretched detached.
Hope-filled spirit,
outreaching, enfolding,
responding to the
lover, palpably,
insatiably, fully.
In simple prayer with
abandon, with no
recourse, in loving
trust, I offer all.
Take me, O Lord.

Going to the Father

The pledge of Christ to me,
a wealth of deeds to see,
and even greater things
to glorify the Father.

Expectantly I pray,
that night will yield to day,
when Christ will be the way
that leads me to the Father.

The sacred moment known,
a time when seed was sown
to fall on fertile ground,
a harvest for the Father.

I've known a saint's reply,
to suffer or to die.
There is a reason why.
I'm going to the Father.

With open stance, you ask,
what role to play, what task?
To be a trusting child;
we are going to the Father.

"Now
we see indistinctly,
as in a mirror;

then
we shall see face to face."

1 Cor. 13:12

The Hidden Face of God

To God whose Face I seek:
You know me and I am.

> I know you and I become.

You see me in the clown-image
    I leave in others' eyes.

> I see you in the transient clouds
>   that form on a summer day.

You hear me in my voiceless
    cry to be whole.

> I hear you in the notes of a
>   Mozart concerto.

You smell me in the odor of tears,
    the moisture of a smile.

> I smell you as bloodhounds
>   their prey.

You feel me in the embraces I give
    the "anawim."

> I feel you in the caress of
>   a woman's hand.

You pronounce me "good" in
    my nakedness.

> I pronounce you "Abba" in
>   your empowering.

You touch me in my innermost self,
    ravishing me, preparing me for love.

> I touch you in Eucharist,
>   ratifying the covenant.

You love me by dying for me.

> I love you by living for you.

"Listen,
my faithful children;

open up your petals,
like roses
planted
near
running
waters."

Sir. 39:13

Nonetheless a Rose

Cascading
    down
like snow of winter's scene,
the roses
    fall,
a flower shower sent from heaven's gate,
whose fragrance fill ours lives and celebrates
the praise of Saint Therese.

Receiving one and wholly unforeseen,
a different type or color than we hoped
or even one in early stage of growth,
a bud or bloom,
but nonetheless a rose.

Some can't be touched or felt,
a spirit thing,
no petals seen, no stem,
a mystery shown in form of beauty, grace
and all that's known of flowers grown,
but nonetheless a rose.

Another view reveals to you
a rose can be a poem, love, a favor sought,
a friendship, children, nothing you'd have thought;
still down it falls,
but nonetheless a rose.

At times denied, but really not refused,
it's saved for you or comes at later date,
or handed on with love to one
with greater cross to bear
but nonetheless a rose.

A rose has thorns which surely can confuse
for gift received is oft perceived
as trial sent to test our faith,
since spirits wane when thorns cause pain,
but nonetheless a rose.

In time we learn our Saint's concern
pertains to us as well
and so from roses raised by us
we pluck a rose
      and then disclose
            it's one we chose
but nonetheless a rose.

An added lesson we can learn from this,
for Sirach writes as he invites
to praise the Lord above,
"My children, give a heed
and blossom like a rose that grows
on bank of running stream";
and be like Christ who rose.

"The glory of Lebanon
will be given to them,
the splendor
of Carmel and Sharon."
Is. 35:2

Carmel's Call

Dormant bushes flourish near
a desert wadi gurgling clear
this starry night,
as doves dismiss the pilgrims' rest
with songs that hint of love possessed,
a sheer delight,
a setting couched in space and time,
to journey risking all to climb
the mountain's height.

The Call to Carmel

"Now summon all Israel to me on Mount Carmel . . . "

1 Kings 18:19

The call to Carmel is linked closely with two historical figures—the prophet Elijah of the Old Testament, and Mary, the Blessed Virgin, Our Lady of Mount Carmel, in the New Testament—and with a place, Mount Carmel, a mountain range in the desert wilderness of Israel. These are the basis of the traditions of Carmel.

The earliest Carmelites were hermits, all living on Mount Carmel, who petitioned Albert, the Patriarch of Jerusalem, for a rule of life, which they received sometime in the period 1206-1214. These men dwelt in solitude on Carmel near the well of Elijah. They celebrated Eucharist daily in a chapel in their midst dedicated to Our Lady. It was only years later that circumstances would force their return to Europe, where they would live as mendicants.

Since that time the desert has been an important symbol in Carmelite life. It is in the harsh reality of the desert that we are stripped of all our belongings and our very selves and there encounter God as did the prophet Elijah before us. In this setting Mount Carmel also plays an important role. It is the journey up this mountain that has been symbolized so well by the Carmelite spiritual doctor St. John of the Cross in his works "The Ascent of Mt. Carmel" and "The Dark Night of the Soul." We risk all in faith to climb that sacred mountain. The resolve to do so requires a leap in faith, a fiat uttered as Our Lady did at the time of the Annunciation.

Yet the physical desert and the mountain are not possible for most of us. Like the Carmelites of medieval times, we live in urban areas among God's people doing our daily work and trying to fill up our days with love. We might be fortunate to journey up some mountain in the West or walk in some desert area of the Southwest. That, however, is free time, only a pause in our daily rounds to nourish and strengthen us by the experience. We might, therefore, ask, In what ways can we encounter the desert and mountain symbolism in Carmelite life?

They are images that became symbols for part of our spiritual journey. The desert is where we encounter God, where God strips us of all that is not of Him, so that we can encounter Him in naked faith. The meeting is a contemplative touch, painful, yet full of love. The mountain stands for the goal of the journey: union with God. This union is capable of ever greater increase and so in that sense is a process. Unlike the early Carmelites who lived in the desert wilderness of Mount Carmel, we carry our desert and mountain within us, wherever we go, wherever a Carmelite lives in space and time.

The desert is a barren place. Existence there is harsh, and only the heartiest of plants and animals can live there. The water needed to sustain life is scarce. The air dehydrates your very being. Without water, a person could die within the space of a few hours on a summer day. Plants that survive in the desert have developed the capacity to subsist on little water, mainly conserving it well by their makeup. Many of them go into a dormant stage between rainfalls.

Yet the desert is alive. Water makes it flourish and turns it green. Everything comes to life after a rain. The desert washes run again, pulsating with life-giving water. Dormant plants, cacti and bushes revitalize and in many cases blossom. It is a scene of beauty when this occurs.

The same process happens to us in our spiritual life. When our interior being dries up for lack of nourishment, existence is harsh and demanding. In order to survive, we must rid ourselves of all non-essentials, those possessions and attitudes formerly thought so necessary to our life. In our confrontation with God in contemplation, we see that they are not necessary for the journey up the mountain. In poverty we encounter our nothingness.

This realization in humility—that we depend on everything from God—enables God to fill us with His spirit, his life, so that we become alive in Jesus Christ. "The life I live now is not my own; Christ is living in me. I still live my human life, but it is a life of faith in the Son of God, who loved me and gave himself for me" (Gal. 2:20).

Another symbol St. John of the Cross highlighted in his works is that of "night." In the night of the soul, God is present to us in a very close fashion. However, we are unable to see Him, because we walk by faith alone. This felt experience of God's absence is seen as darkness. Yet in reality it is God flooding us with His presence. Paradoxically, we are able during this night to see many things clearly, things light prevented us from seeing before: such growth-producing realities as greater self-knowledge, our dependence on God and the ability to have great desires. It is as in the desert sky, where the stars are seen very clearly, producing a beautiful sky picture.

The "night" is a love encounter with our God. We feel His absence, and yet He is very present to us, loving us, transforming us into the image of His Son. He conceals Himself to deepen our faith as we look for Him. His felt absence increases our desire for more encounters, having been touched by His grace.

Therefore, the call to Carmel is an invitation to intimacy with the Lord, making God the center of our lives, forsaking created things, ultimately to experience them in God. It is an offer to journey up Mount Carmel, where we encounter deeply the living God. As our love grows strong, the Song of Songs in the Old Testament becomes one of the dominant themes in our lives with its imagery of the mutual love between a groom and his bride, symbolizing the love of Christ and the individual soul. "My lover speaks; he says to me/ 'Arise, my beloved, my beautiful one,/ and come!/ For see, the winter is past,/ the rains are over and gone./ The flowers appear on the earth,/ the time of pruning the vines has come,/ and the song of the dove is heard in our land' " (Songs 2:10-12).

All this, however, is in promise. It is not yet. The promise can be realized one day, since the call to Carmel has been made and answered. Yet there are many years when we must form community, render ministry and achieve closeness to God through prayer. It would be nice if we could spend all our days on Mount Carmel, living there in solitude with the God whom we love. This is not possible, and so the desert with its mountain must be within our hearts, teaching us its lessons in times of dryness and of night as it nourishes us when the rain falls from heaven.

Also there is no chapel for us to Our Lady in the midst of all the hermits where we can sing Mary's praise. There is only her call to us to answer Yes to the divine action in our lives as she did when she uttered her fiat, in order that we might become, like her, Christ-bearers.

This process has continued over the last eight centuries wherever people have responded to the call of Carmel. It is a labor of a lifetime, a work of love. In faith and trust, we surrender everything that is not God, so that God can be all in us. It happens not in desert oases, where beautiful plants grow amid plentiful water, but in the midst of our cities, where life is hectic and hurried, and where we, like the prophet Elijah, are called to do battle with the false prophets of our day. That is Carmel's challenge: to preserve the desert in the midst of the cities, a challenge that began when the first Carmelites migrated to Europe. It continues today.